ENGLISH SMOCKS

With directions and patterns for making them

Alice Armes

Dryad Press Ltd   London

© Dryad Press Ltd 1987
Eighth edition first published 1977
Reprinted 1980

Ninth edition first published 1987

ISBN 0 8521 9657 1

Typeset by Tek-Art Ltd, Kent
and printed by David Green Printers Ltd,
Kettering, Northants
for the Publishers
Dryad Press Limited,
8 Cavendish Square,
London W1M 0AJ

front cover: *smock made to pattern number 8
(Staffordshire and Shropshire Gardener)
by Pat Gibson, Beech Hill Rd., Sunningdale.*

The word smock is of Anglo-Saxon derivation meaning a 'Shift' or 'Chemise', and it is from these days that the smock of rural England dates. The Anglo-Saxon shift in its first stage was a plain shirt-like garment without fullness, but apparently it soon developed a certain amount of gathering in the front and back owing to the need of extra width in a garment worn by men engaged in occupations of a strenuous nature.

A picture of the time of Charles I is the first record we have illustrating a full smock, but it is not possible to see whether the gathers are controlled by stitchery. It will be seen by this that smocking is one of the few peasant crafts which we have in England and that owing to its practical use as well as its beauty it has been carried on for hundreds of years. Up to eighty years ago the smock was in general use in the rural districts of England and its disappearance was obviously due to the introduction of machine-looms which produced inexpensive materials and enabled country workers to procure clothing at a comparatively small cost with the minimum amount of trouble. That English smocks should become extinct is greatly to be regretted for they are practical and beautiful garments which would still serve a very useful as well as decorative purpose.

It may be some time before men will take to wearing smocks again, but now that the field of work open to women is widened and they are becoming more practical in their dress, there is reason to believe that there may again arise a demand for beautiful smocks.

A few isolated cases of men wearing smocks have been noted recently, namely, a shepherd driving his sheep to Leighton Buzzard market, an old man in Sussex, and another playing a whistle in the streets of Reading wore a good Berkshire smock. In a village in Sussex smocks are still worn at funerals by the bearers. The wearing of smocks was general in all the agricultural districts of England and Wales, and a good many still exist in the Southern and Midland Counties, but those of the North seem to have disappeared, though they are known to have been worn as far North as Durham and Yorkshire.

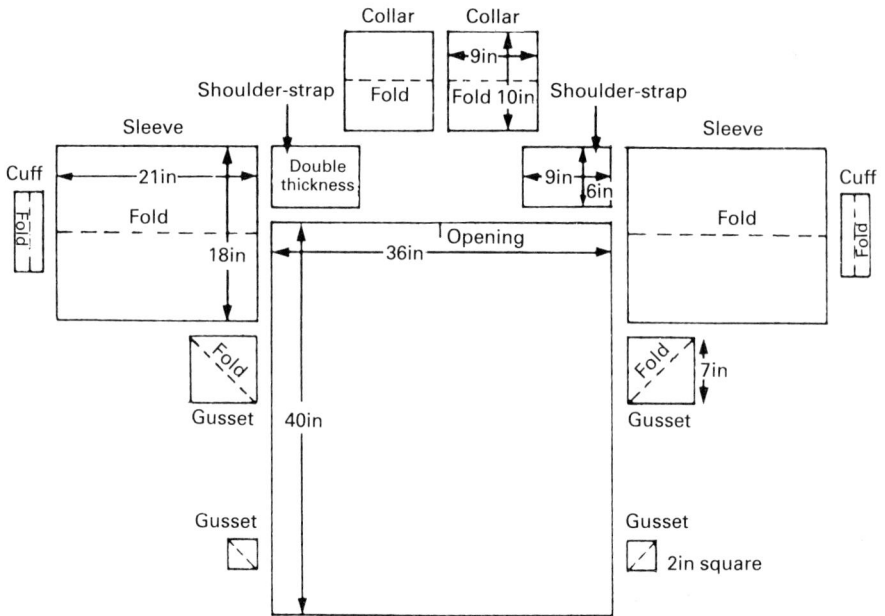

Collar
Collar
Shoulder-strap
Shoulder-strap
Sleeve
Sleeve
Cuff
Cuff
Fold
9in
Fold 10in
21in
Double thickness
9in
6in
Fold
Fold
Fold
Fold
18in
Opening
36in
Fold
Fold
Gusset
40in
Gusset
7in
Gusset
Gusset
2in square

Diagram 1.
A Smock cut out

The number and position of the various parts of a smock are shown, but they must NOT be placed on the material in this way for cutting out

The Construction or 'Cut'

Several varieties of 'cut' in smocks were used, the most general being that which was reversible, for the back and front were alike with a small opening at the neck to allow the wearer to pull it easily over his head; secondly, that which opened like a coat from neck to hem with a square cut collar, shallow at the back and extending to such width on the shoulder that it reached nearly to the elbow; this pattern was worn in Kent and Hereford while in Yorkshire a short smock set into a band round the hips prevailed. In all cases the cut of smocks was of the utmost simplicity, the component parts were entirely squares and oblongs; curves were never introduced in cutting a smock, so they are a perfect example of simple construction and utility.

Many of the old workers planned a smock entirely by folding and cutting the material in the following manner: the length required from neck to hem was taken and three times this length of material was required. It was then folded into three equal lengths, two of which formed the back and front of the smock; the third piece was again folded into three, two pieces for the sleeves and the third piece made the collar, gussets and shoulder straps. In diagram No. 1 the squares and oblongs for the smock are shown when cut out.

Diagram 2 shows a completed smock with the names of the various parts.

Pockets when included in a smock were of two kinds: (1) the 'inset' placed in the side seam, and (2) that with 'lid' or 'flap'; this was always placed across the side seam so that in each case the smock could be worn either way round, but in a great many instances an opening was left in the side seam so that the wearer could use his breeches pocket instead.

Colour   The colour of the smocks varied in different counties. White or natural were generally worn in Berkshire, Hampshire, Wiltshire, and the counties round about

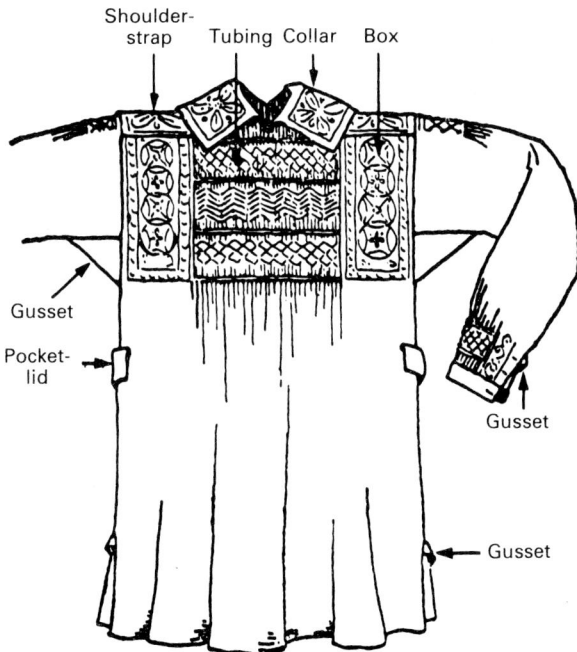

Diagram 2. Smock with various parts named

Shoulder-strap   Tubing   Collar   Box

Gusset

Pocket-lid

Gusset

Gusset

London; in Hertfordshire, Essex and Cambridge an olive-green was the work-day smock; in the Midlands, viz., Leicestershire, Derby, Nottingham and Stafford, a deep blue smock called a 'Newark Frock' was worn; black smocks worked in white were found in Surrey, and the Isle of Wight, and in many counties a drab or grey was the colour of the everday smock. In every county the best or Sunday smock was made of white linen worked with white. In several counties blue was the colour adopted by the shepherds and in Dorset the drab smocks were often worked in two colours, viz., blue and white, a variety not found elsewhere. In Sussex, noted for its elaborate smocks, drab or grey with white for best were the rule.

Materials The material used for smocks naturally had to be of a very durable nature, and they were made of such wear-resisting materials as hemp and flax. In Shakespeare's time we read of the hempen homespun smock and the white smocks were generally of handspun hand-woven linen. A strong twilled material called 'drabbette' was much used, but owing to its stiffness and unyielding nature it was not employed for the full smocks and was more suitable for the plainer coat-shaped smocks. When the wearing of smocks was on the decline, this material was bought up by a firm in London, who recognised its wonderful wearing qualities and from it made their famous waterproofs.

Generally strong twisted linen thread was used for working smocks, and for the very thick varieties of material the thread was used double in the needle, but in some counties ordinary sewing cotton was substituted.

Decoration or Embroidery Elaborately decorated smocks were not produced before the middle of the eighteenth century, and they reached their greatest perfection in the early part of the nineteenth century. It has been stated that the patterns worked on the smocks

(text continued on page 13)

1. Woodman's Smock. Photograph reproduced by kind permission of
the Victoria and Albert Museum, S. Kensington

2. Shepherd's Smock, Nottinghamshire. Made of deep blue linen
worked with thick thread of a deeper shade of blue. Photograph
reproduced by kind permission of Castle Museum, Nottingham

3. Essex Shepherd's Smock, made of dull green linen worked with brown linen thread

4. Shepherd's Smock, Warwickshire, white linen

5. English Smock, first half of 19th century. Brown linen. Reproduced by
kind permission of the Victoria and Albert Museum

6. Gardener's Smock, Staffordshire. White linen. This pattern was also
used in Shropshire

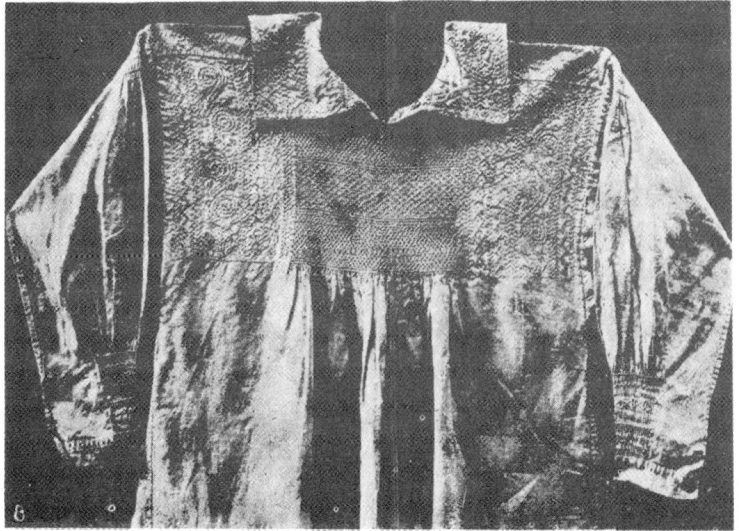

7. Detail patterns from Dorset Woodman's Smock

8. A Bedfordshire Smock

9 and 10. Patterns from Smocks of various counties

11

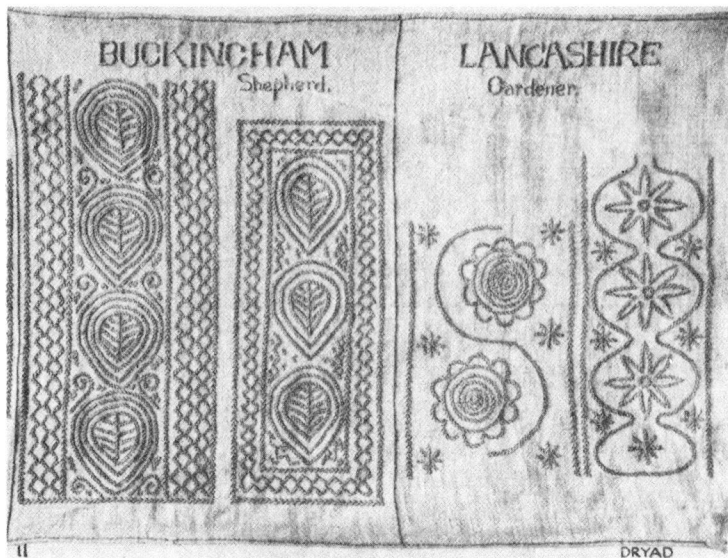

11 and 12. Patterns from Smocks of various counties

varied in different counties, and that each county had its own traditional designs, but it is more likely that the variety of patterns was used to distinguish the various trades of the wearers and that the same designs were common to many counties. These designs from their simplicity appear in most cases to have been worked directly on to the smock without previous drawing and were made up of very simple units.

It is not known precisely at what date the embroidery was introduced on the collar, front and back of the smocks, but the designs used definitely denote the trade of the wearer. In Dorset and possibly also in other counties, farmers at 'hirings' looked at the men's smocks to find out the trade of the wearers.

The embroidery in which emblems of the trades were used was placed on the plain piece of material on either side of the 'tubing' or gathering on the smock and was called the 'box' except in the case of the coat-shaped smock, when it was placed on the wide collar instead. The designs for the various trades generally included conventionalised representations of the following emblems, though they are sometimes rather difficult to decipher.

Waggoners or Carters   Cart-wheels, whip lashes, reins and bits.
Woodmen   Trees and leaves.
Gardeners   Flowers and leaves.
Shepherds   Crooks, sheep-pens, hurdles and sheep.
Milkmaids   Churns, butter-pats, hearts, etc.
A Gravedigger's smock had crosses.
Butchers' smocks are somewhat difficult to decipher and one can only surmise that the objects in the Shropshire butcher's smock represent chopping-blocks, saws and pounds of meat.

Full sized patterns of decoration for smocks will be found in the pockets at the ends of this book.

Stitches   The stitches employed in the construction and decoration of smocks were of the simplest description such as feather-stitching, single, double and treble, for

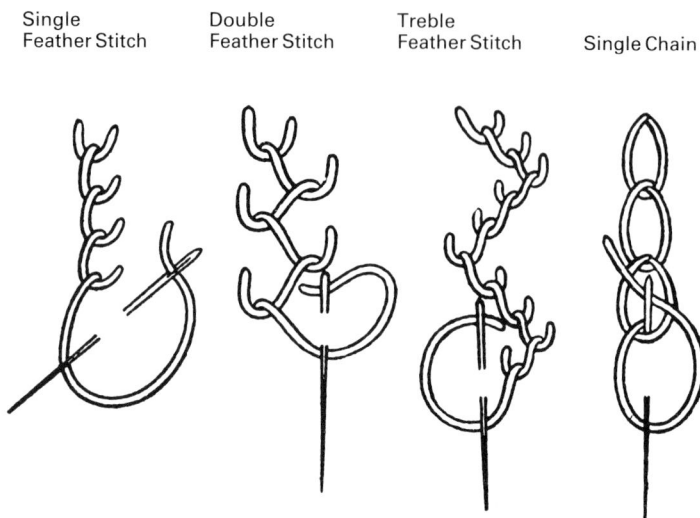

| Single
Feather Stitch | Double
Feather Stitch | Treble
Feather Stitch | Single Chain |

Diagram 3

the embroidery, though occasionally chain-stitch, faggot-stitch, stem-stitch and satin-stitch were used, while practically the only stitch used on the 'tubing' was 'stem' or 'outline' stitch in different combinations and proportions. (See diagram 3). The successful results obtained from these simple stitches is due to regular working and even tension, the latter being a most important point.

The introduction of various embroidery stitches on modern smocks, far from improving their appearance, has produced work lacking the richness and charm of the older specimens, just as the introduction of curves in the cut has detracted from the beauty which in the original smocks came from their valuable straight lines.

How to make a Smock   The most suitable material for a smock is undoubtedly a well-woven linen, preferably of natural colour as it will not have been weakened by bleaching or dyeing; it should be worked with stout twisted linen thread, such as D.M.C. linen lace thread, or if a cheaper make is required, Knox's unbleached unglazed carpet thread, though this is not so evenly spun. If a cotton material is used it should be worked with dull-finish embroidery cotton; mercerised cottons are not suitable, and an invariable rule is that linen should be worked with linen, and cotton should be used on cotton.

For a man's smock 4 yds (3.65m) of material not less than 36in (914mm) wide will be required if a fairly heavy quality is used. If a light weight or thin material is used a wider width is better as it naturally gathers up into smaller compass.

First the two oblong pieces which form the body of the smock should be cut; these generally measure about 36in (914mm) wide and 40in (1m 16mm) long. The sleeves also are oblongs about 21in (533mm) long × 18in (457mm) wide, set into narrow cuff bands of double material. The back and front of the smock are connected by two shoulder straps or yokes of double material, measuring 8in (203mm) to 9in (229mm) from neck to shoulder and about 6in (153mm) wide, according to the requirements of the wearer. A small opening is made in the centre of the back and front of the neck of the smock to allow for the wearer pulling it over his head.

The collar is also open back and front, and is of double material, each piece measuring 9in (229mm) long and 5in (127mm) deep when folded.

Four square gussets are required; two measuring 7in (178mm) square folded diagonally are let into the under-arm seam of the sleeve to give ample play to the wearer. The side seam of the skirt is left open for 2in (51mm) or 3in (76mm) at the base, and a small gusset 2in (51mm) square is inserted in the same way as in the sleeve.

The smock being cut out, it is as well first to embroider the 'box' before 'tubing' or gathering the front and back. The base of the 'box' should be level with the under-arm seam of the sleeve, and this horizontal line should also terminate the stitchery on the tubing. The width of the 'box' should be half or slightly more than half that of the tubing when complete. A tacking thread of coloured cotton should mark the boundary of the tubing on either side, and should be run in carefully following the thread of the warp of the material. The smock is then ready to be 'tubed' back and front and the importance of exercising the greatest care and accuracy over this cannot be too strongly emphasised for on it depends the elasticity which is essential to a good smock. The gathering threads should be run in by the thread of the material, and no dots, transfers or marks should be used; the beginner is therefore advised to use a material in which the threads can easily be seen. The use of transfers is to be condemned, for they are seldom evenly printed, and it is exceedingly difficult to iron them on to the material on line with the thread and if the gathering threads do not follow the thread of the material, the smock will hang crooked.

None of the old skilful smockers used dots for they soon acquired the knack of gathering straight 'by eye', and once the habit is acquired it is a much quicker and infinitely superior method. Very strong cotton or thread must be used for the gathering and the ends must be securely fastened off, this being the only occasion on which a good knot may be used in smocking. After knotting the thread it should be marked with pencil at the point at which it is to be finished off, generally about 4in (102mm) to 4½in (114mm) for the front or back, and this will ensure every row being drawn up to exactly the same length. The gathers or reeds should be drawn up closely so that when they are finally stitched they form a firm compact series of regular tubes. Allowance must be made for the space which the embroidery thread will take up between the reeds. The rows of gathering should not be more than ½in (13mm) apart, and the stitches should be of equal length on both sides of the material, also the line of stitches must be kept vertically as well as horizontally.

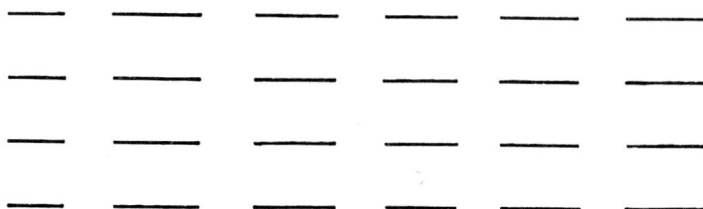

The rows of gathering should begin ½in (13mm) from the upper edge of the material and extend to at least 1in (25mm) below the base of the stitchery, and each row should be started from the right side. The embroidery must be started from the left side. It is important that in making up a smock the reeds should be kept true into the collar, shoulder-straps and wrist-bands. The stitches used on the tubing which really are all varieties of one kind of stitch, are three in number, viz., Rope, Basket and Chevron. These stitches are practically the stitch generally known as stem-stitch.

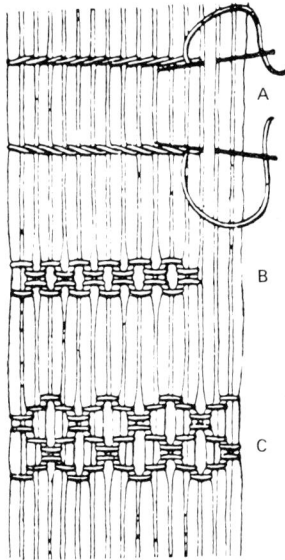

Diagram 4

Rope, diagram 4A, is a line of stem-stitch worked from reed to reed, taking a small piece of the material on the needle. It can be used in single, double or treble lines in one direction only, or in alternate lines in each direction. The top and base of the tubing should always begin and end with two or three lines of Rope as this gives the greatest strength, and in the old smocks one or two lines worked close together were generally used to separate the blocks of 'Basket' and 'Chevron'.

Basket, diagram 4B, is formed by working two lines of outline stitch or rope in one journey, throwing the thread alternately to the right and left of the needle when working across; it will be seen in the diagram that the upper stitch in the second row of Basket is on the same reeds as the lower stitch of the first row.

Chevron, diagram 4C, again is outline stitch worked in steps to form chevrons, and a great variety of effects may be obtained by different groupings. In working chevron stitch, care must be taken to keep the stitches at right angles to the reeds; the throwing the thread to the right or left of the needle governs the direction of the chevron or zig-zag. These are the only kinds of stitch used on the *tubing* of old smocks and such stitches as feather-stitch, honeycomb, etc., are modern innovations not to be recommended. The only knot permissible in the stitchery on the tubing is at the beginning of each row, so the worker must put enough thread in her needle to complete the stitchery right across. Knots in any other part of the tubing denote bad workmanship and cause unevenness in the reeds.

The stitchery being completed, the tacking threads are removed, and the tubing will then be found to be beautifully elastic, and so give to the movements of the wearer. It is this elasticity which makes smocks such suitable garments for growing children.

The fullness at the top and wrist of the sleeve is tubed and worked in exactly the same way as the body of the smock. The embroidery on the collar should be worked through *one* thickness of the material only, before the collar is folded and made up.

In the same way the embroidery on the shoulder strap should be worked before it is attached to the garment, and the under thickness hemmed neatly on to it aftrwards.

In making up a smock, it is advisable:

1. To join the back and front together by the shoulder-strap.

2. To set on the collar.

3. Sew in the sleeve as far as the gusset; for this a run and fell seam should be used.

4. Join the side seam leaving space for the under-arm gusset and pocket if the latter is to be inset. If the edges are selvedges they should be seamed on the wrong side, and if one or both are cut edges the run and fell seam is used.

5. Set in under-arm gussets with run and fell seam, also the small gussets into the skirt in the same way as those in a man's shirt.

On the old smocks we find various kinds of button from bone to the brass trouser button, but the most suitable and satisfactory seem to be the old dorset 'cart-wheel' variety.

Little mention has been made of the actual designs to be used on the boxes and collars of smocks as it is felt that from the pictures and designs from old smocks which are here given, the worker of today will be able to select or evolve those suitable for her own purpose and it is suggested that our embroiderers, spinners, weavers, potters and other craftspeople, by producing and wearing smocks, might revive one of the most beautiful of old English crafts.